CW00602450

First published by Bloomsbury Books
an imprint of The Godfrey Cave Group
42 Bloomsbury Street
London WC1B 3QJ

© The Godfrey Cave Group, 1993
© Lys de Bray (all illustrations), original copyright 1983,
renewed in 1991 and 1993

ISBN 1 85471 108 3

All rights reserved. No part of this publication may be
reproduced, stored in a retrieval system, or transmitted in any
form or by any means, electronic, mechanical, photocopying,
recording or otherwise, without the prior permission of the
copyright owner.

Conceived and designed by Savitri Books Ltd
115J Cleveland Street
London W1P 5PN

Printed and bound in Great Britain by
BPCC Hazells Ltd
Member of BPCC Ltd

The illustrations contained in this daybook are the work
of Lys de Bray and first appeared in 1983 in her book,
Cottage Garden Year, which was republished in 1991.
Lys de Bray is the author of some ten books and devotes
her time to writing and painting, and to tending
her much loved garden.

COTTAGE GARDEN

Lys de Bray

DAYBOOK

Bloomsbury Books
London

January

1	
2	
3	

Garden tasks in January

_____
_____
_____
_____
_____
_____
_____
_____
_____
_____
_____
_____
_____
_____
_____
_____
_____
_____
_____
_____
_____
_____
_____
_____

OBSERVATIONS _____
_____
_____
_____
_____

JANUARY

4

5

6

7

8

9

10

Winter Jasmine

11

12

13

14

15

16

17

Viburnum bodnantense 'Dawn'

JANUARY

18

19

20

21

22

23

24

Helleborus foetidus

JANUARY

| 25 |
| 26 |
| 27 |
| 28 |
| 29 |
| 30 |
| 31 |

Hedera helix canariensis 'variegata' 'Gloire de Marengo'

February

1

2

3

Garden tasks in February

_____
_____
_____
_____
_____
_____
_____
_____
_____
_____
_____
_____
_____
_____
_____
_____
_____
_____
_____
_____
_____
_____
_____
_____
_____
_____

OBSERVATIONS _____
_____
_____
_____
_____

FEBRUARY

4

5

6

7

8

9

10

Crocus aureus

FEBRUARY

| 11 |
| 12 |
| 13 |
| 14 |
| 15 |
| 16 |
| 17 |

Cymbidium

FEBRUARY

| 18 |
| 19 |
| 20 |
| 21 |
| 22 |
| 23 |
| 24 |

Mahonia japonica

FEBRUARY

25
26
27
28/29

Crocus 'Remembrance'

March

1

2

3

Garden tasks in March

_____
_____
_____
_____
_____
_____
_____
_____
_____
_____
_____
_____
_____
_____
_____
_____
_____
_____
_____
_____
_____
_____
_____

OBSERVATIONS _____
_____
_____
_____
_____

MARCH

4

5

6

7

8

9

10

Crown Imperial

MARCH

11

12

13

14

15

16

17

Purple Deadnettle

MARCH

18

19

20

21

22

23

24

Yellow Tulip 'Bellona'

MARCH

25
26
27
28
29
30
31

Lungwort

April

1

2

3

Garden tasks in April

_____
_____
_____
_____
_____
_____
_____
_____
_____
_____
_____
_____
_____
_____
_____
_____
_____
_____
_____
_____
_____
_____
_____
_____

OBSERVATIONS _____
_____
_____
_____
_____

APRIL

4
5
6
7
8
9
10

Pasque Flower

APRIL

11	
12	
13	
14	
15	
16	
17	

Clematis macropetala 'Blue Lagoon'

APRIL

18

19

20

21

22

23

24

Wallflowers

APRIL

25	
26	
27	
28	
29	
30	

Scots Pine

May

1

2

3

Garden tasks in May

_____
_____
_____
_____
_____
_____
_____
_____
_____
_____
_____
_____
_____
_____
_____
_____
_____
_____
_____
_____
_____
_____
_____
_____
_____

OBSERVATIONS _____
_____
_____
_____
_____

MAY

4

5

6

7

8

9

10

Ground Ivy

11

12

13

14

15

16

17

Lily of the Valley

MAY

18

19

20

21

22

23

24

Monkshood

MAY

| 25 |
| 26 |
| 27 |
| 28 |
| 29 |
| 30 |
| 31 |

Pinks

1	
2	
3	

Garden tasks in June

_____
_____
_____
_____
_____
_____
_____
_____
_____
_____
_____
_____
_____
_____
_____
_____
_____
_____
_____
_____
_____
_____
_____
_____

OBSERVATIONS _____
_____
_____
_____
_____

JUNE

4	
5	
6	
7	
8	
9	
10	

Rose 'Zambra'

JUNE

11
12
13
14
15
16
17

Iris sibrica

JUNE

18
19
20
21
22
23
24

Clematis 'Ville de Lyon'

JUNE

25

26

27

28

29

30

Rose Campion

July

1

2

3

Garden tasks in July

_____
_____
_____
_____
_____
_____
_____
_____
_____
_____
_____
_____
_____
_____
_____
_____
_____
_____
_____
_____
_____
_____
_____

OBSERVATIONS _____
_____
_____
_____
_____

JULY

| 4 |
| 5 |
| 6 |
| 7 |
| 8 |
| 9 |
| 10 |

Sweet William

JULY

11
12
13
14
15
16
17

Canterbury Bell

JULY

18

19

20

21

22

23

24

Cornflower

JULY

25

26

27

28

29

30

31

Fuchsia 'Little Fellow'

August

1	
2	
3	

Garden tasks in August

_____
_____
_____
_____
_____
_____
_____
_____
_____
_____
_____
_____
_____
_____
_____
_____
_____
_____
_____
_____
_____
_____
_____
_____
_____
_____
_____

OBSERVATIONS _____
_____
_____
_____
_____

AUGUST

4

5

6

7

8

9

10

Pelargonium 'Mrs Henry Cox'

AUGUST

| 11 |
| 12 |
| 13 |
| 14 |
| 15 |
| 16 |
| 17 |

Elecampane

AUGUST

18	
19	
20	
21	
22	
23	
24	

Nasturtium

AUGUST

25

26

27

28

29

30

31

Cosmea

September

1

2

3

Garden tasks in September

_____
_____
_____
_____
_____
_____
_____
_____
_____
_____
_____
_____
_____
_____
_____
_____
_____
_____
_____
_____
_____
_____
_____
_____

OBSERVATIONS _____
_____
_____
_____

SEPTEMBER

4

5

6

7

8

9

10

Broad Bean

SEPTEMBER

11

12

13

14

15

16

17

Clematis orientalis 'Lemon Peel'

SEPTEMBER

18

19

20

21

22

23

24

Honeysuckle

SEPTEMBER

| 25 |
| 26 |
| 27 |
| 28 |
| 29 |
| 30 |

Myrtle

October

1

2

3

Garden tasks in October

_____
_____
_____
_____
_____
_____
_____
_____
_____
_____
_____
_____
_____
_____
_____
_____
_____
_____
_____
_____
_____
_____
_____
_____
_____

OBSERVATIONS _____
_____
_____
_____
_____

OCTOBER

4

5

6

7

8

9

10

Dahlia

OCTOBER

11

12

13

14

15

16

17

Hips of Dog Rose

OCTOBER

18

19

20

21

22

23

24

Guelder Rose

OCTOBER

25

26

27

28

29

30

31

Hips of Rose Cupid

November

1

2

3

Garden tasks in November

_____
_____
_____
_____
_____
_____
_____
_____
_____
_____
_____
_____
_____
_____
_____
_____
_____
_____
_____
_____
_____
_____
_____
_____
_____
_____
_____

OBSERVATIONS _____
_____
_____
_____
_____

NOVEMBER

4
5
6
7
8
9
10

Parrotia persica

NOVEMBER

| 11 |
| 12 |
| 13 |
| 14 |
| 15 |
| 16 |
| 17 |

Common Polypody

NOVEMBER

18	
19	
20	
21	
22	
23	
24	

Common Ivy

25

26

27

28

29

30

Iris foetidissima

December

1

2

3

Garden tasks in December

_____
_____
_____
_____
_____
_____
_____
_____
_____
_____
_____
_____
_____
_____
_____
_____
_____
_____
_____
_____
_____
_____
_____
_____
_____
_____

OBSERVATIONS _____
_____
_____
_____
_____

DECEMBER

4

5

6

7

8

9

10

Hedera helix canariensis 'variegata'
Gloire de Marengo

DECEMBER

11	
12	
13	
14	
15	
16	
17	

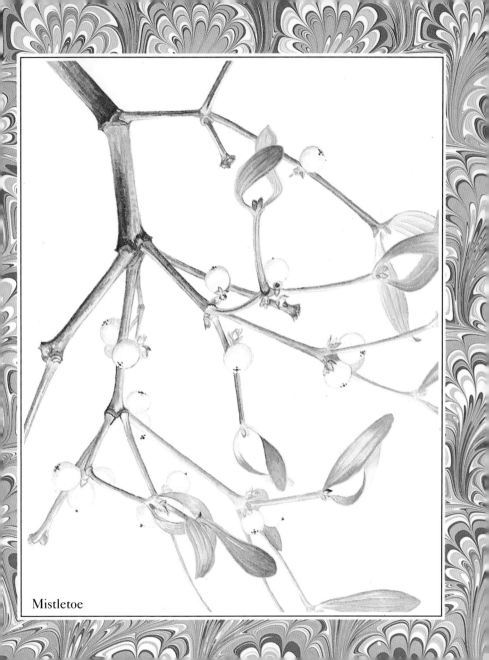

Mistletoe

DECEMBER

18

19

20

21

22

23

24

Christmas Rose

DECEMBER

25

26

27

28

29

30

31

Holly